Communion Meditations and Prayers

Laurence C. Keene
Kenton K. Smith
Russ Blowers

STANDARD PUBLISHING
Cincinnati, Ohio

Except where otherwise noted, Scripture quotations are from the *King James Version* of the Bible.

Scripture quotations from the *New International Version* of the Bible are copyright © 1978, New York International Bible Society.

Library of Congress Cataloging in Publication Data

    Keene, Laurence C.
      Communion meditations and prayers.

      1. Lord's Supper—Meditations. I. Smith, Kenton K. II. Blowers, Russell F. III. Title.
    BV826.5.K43   264   81-16668
    ISBN 0-87239-483-2   AACR2

Copyright © 1982, The STANDARD PUBLISHING Company, Cincinnati, Ohio.
A division of STANDEX INTERNATIONAL Corporation.
Printed in U.S.A.

Contents

Foreword 5
Communion Meditations
  (Keene) 9
  (Smith) 58
  (Blowers) 85
Meditations for Special Days
  (Keene) 115

Foreword

Each element of worship—the singing, the prayers, the giving of our tithes and offerings, the sermon—has its special place and meaning for the worshiper. But to many of us the quiet moment when we privately commune with God during the "breaking of bread" is the most inwardly meaningful part of the worship service.

One of the difficulties the busy minister or elder faces is the task of providing fresh and inspirational insight each week in guiding the worshiper through this meaningful part of the worship service. It is our hope that these Communion meditations will be helpful to those who are called to lead in worship at the table.

Each meditation is accompanied with a Scripture reading and prayer that reflect the theme and content of the meditation. The leader is free to incorporate as much or as little of each Sunday's meditation as he deems best.

Some of the Communion meditations are written to reflect the major sacred and secular holidays of the year. Others have been based upon hymns that are often sung during the Communion service. (The hymn numbers listed are those in *Favorite Hymns of Praise*.) In this way it is hoped that the hymns we sing and the holidays we celebrate will also be used to exalt the Christ whom we encounter in the breaking of bread.

The general church membership may also find some value in obtaining their own personal copies of this book, to guide them in their private devotion around the Lord's table.

Communion Meditations

Keeping and Losing

Scripture Reading: Matthew 16:24, 25

The Christian life is an attempt to lose that which we cannot keep, and gain that which we cannot lose!

We wish to lose ourselves in dedication to God, for we know we cannot keep our lives forever. We seek to gain a place in God's kingdom that no man can take from us.

This is God's plan of "give and take"! We recognize this plan in marriage, in business, and in every walk of life. What we get out of life depends upon what we are willing to give.

At the table of the Lord it is a frequent temptation to give God our troubles, our worries, our sins, our guilt, and everything else but what He wants. And what He really wants is us! "Seek ye first the kingdom of God . . . and all these things shall be added unto you."

We can paraphrase Jesus' words by saying: "Give up what you cannot keep, so you can gain that which you cannot ever lose!"

Prayer

Heavenly Father, we do not want to be losers! We have had so much practice at trying to manage things all by ourselves that it is difficult to let go and let You be in charge. It will be hard not to be in control, but give us the victory we need: a victory over the world outside us and over the troublesome world inside us. In Jesus' name, amen.

The Eye of the Beholder

Scripture Reading: Matthew 13:16, 17

The Communion loaf and cup are symbols. An animal can learn to respond to a symbol in a certain way through repeated associations, such as a dog coming to heel when his master whistles. But, aside from God himself, only man can make symbols. Only he can give meaning or change the meaning of a symbol.

Most of us add our own special meaning and significance to the Lord's Supper when we partake. To some, the Lord's Supper represents a mysterious prescription given by the Great Physician to bring healing and relief to their hurts. To others, the Lord's Supper represents a disciplined response to duty: a duty to assemble, to eat, and to pray. Others will find in the Communion service a larger family of which they can claim to be a part, a feeling of largeness and greatness that can help relieve the sense of insignificance that so many feel.

There is value in all these meanings and, of course, in the special meaning *you* bring to this service. These symbols are merely physical elements. It is what *you* add to them that enriches your soul and enables you to walk in Jesus' steps.

Prayer
Our heavenly Father, we all come to this table with different images of You in our minds. Our pictures and thoughts of You are varied and uniquely our own. But in one respect we all feel the same. We are here because we know how incomplete and inadequate we are. We come here in need of a filling—Your filling. In Christ's name, amen.

Coming Clean

Scripture Reading: Psalm 51:10-12

It's a good feeling to come clean. It's a good feeling to know that we are holding nothing back that will cause us to feel blemished within. This is the feeling people often describe following their baptism, a feeling that one has become cleansed—deeply cleansed.

Sooner or later we all have to come clean! To

our wives and husbands, to our parents, to ourselves, and to our God. However, clean things have a way of becoming soiled all over again. People will often find themselves faced again and again with the need to come clean.

Each Sunday the Lord's table provides us with this cleansing opportunity. We have perhaps been taught that we must be clean before we can come to the table, but this is not true at God's table. It is here that we can come clean. The cleansing act is not something we do for ourselves in order that we may see God, but something God does for us because we have seen God! As for our sins and unrighteousness, we "wash our hands" of them right now at God's table!

Prayer

Our Father in Heaven, we have come to church washed and scrubbed and wearing our best clothes. But we know we are not hiding our inner condition from You. Cleanse us this morning so that we will look as good on the inside as we do on the outside. In Jesus' name, **amen.**

Joy to the World

Scripture Reading: John 16:20-24

Peter called it "joy unspeakable and full of glory." He was talking about the Christian experience—the Christian life.

If any word captures the Christian spirit, it is the word "joy." The early Christians would often name their daughters "Karen," the Greek word for *joy*.

However, it is easy to have one's joys dissipated by long hours of working on church committees, preparing church dinners, or by years of service in some official capacity in the church.

The Communion service is designed to help us remove some of the tarnish from forgotten joys. It helps us to remember that "all work and no pray" takes some of the joy out of our Christian experience.

This Communion service shouts to the entire assembly:

Joy to the world,
    the Lord has come!

Prayer

Father, calm us enough now so we can let the joy out. Keep us from feeling self-conscious, so that the joy will continue to flow. Give us good memories so we can remember how good it feels to be joyous. For Your sake, amen.

What's in a Name?

Scripture Reading: Acts 4:10-12

Perhaps we should not refer to God as "Father" any more.

In Jesus' time the father was the master and ruler of the house. He was the provider and the punisher. He would lead and love, reward and chastise. He was the one everyone feared, respected, and looked up to.

Today's father is sometimes seen as the man who has left his wife and children, or the man out of a job and destitute. Sometimes he is aimless. Sometimes he has aimed badly.

This is not the picture of God that Jesus had in mind.

God is always the same, of course, but our definition of Him changes. Words and ideas take on new meaning with the passing of time.

The Lord's Supper helps us clear up our definition and idea of God. If you had a good father, then God is certainly a Father to you. If you've had a good friend, then He's a good Friend to you. If your body has been saved from an experience of sickness and pain, then He's the Good Physician to you. As we discover more about life's demands and its rewards, we also discover more about our heavenly Father. Through the ordinary things of everyday life, we discover the many new ways and names by which God can be known and understood.

Prayer

We know You are above any name we could give You, O God, but we only name You so we can feel closer to You. It is closeness we seek, not titles and names. Enter our hearts completely and fill us with Your presence, so we will know for certain that we are Your children and share in Your good name. In the name of Your Son, Jesus, we pray. Amen.

Bringing Meekness to Supper

Scripture Reading: Proverbs 16:18

After Jesus and His disciples partook of the loaf and the cup at His last supper with them, they sang a hymn together. As they departed, Jesus detained them to give them one last warning: "You will all fall away. When the shepherd is stricken the sheep will be scattered."

Peter replied, "These others perhaps, but not I, Lord."

"You will fall three times before tomorrow's dawn," said Jesus.

It is good for us to remember and reflect on these words as we gather around His table. Many of us have such strong feelings of holiness and goodness that we think, "While other members of the family might fall, I will never fall." Jesus would perhaps say to us that we are never quite as low as when we are feeling important. We are never quite as imperfect as when we consider ourselves to be good. We are never quite as lost as when we boast of our security and safety. Jesus would remind us that meekness, not arrogance, will inherit the earth.

Singing hymns together in church is no guarantee that we will not stumble on the way out. But it is the right place to begin. Every journey begins with the first step. The Communion service is our attempt at putting our best foot forward.

Prayer

Our Father in Heaven, some of us have been very good at putting our foot in our mouth instead of putting it along the right path, where

Jesus walked. Our Monday faith is not always like our Sunday faith. We pray again, as we have many times before, that You would help us be more consistent in our expression of devotion. Keep us from too many highs and lows. Help us to balance our enthusiasm with periods of quiet meditation and contemplation instead of with periods of depression and doubt. In Jesus' name, amen.

Keep the Change

Scripture Reading: Psalm 51:10

"A day late and a dollar short" describes the person who always misses the big deal in life that might have put him on easy street. We have all sometimes been a dollar short or a day late from cashing in on a good thing. Successful living, however, doesn't always depend upon having the correct change or being in the right place at the right time. It usually depends upon great effort and persistence on our part.

This is true of great faith, too. We do not simply fall into it by luck, but rather it filters into us. And usually this happens slowly and with considerable effort and courage on our part.

One begins by nurturing his faith and ends up being nurtured by it. At this table we feed our faith so that later on we might be fed by it.

If you have come to partake of these sacred emblems, you are in the right place at the right time. The only changes you will need to be perfectly happy are a change of heart and a change in your expectations!

Prayer

Thank You, Father, for the changes You have already made in our lives and for the ones You are working on right now! We know we are not quite what we ought to be, but we also know that we are not what we once were. Amen.

Blessings and Disguises

Scripture Reading: John 7:24

Perhaps you have heard people refer to something as a "blessing in disguise." Phyllis Kerr, in her book, *The Snake Has All the Lines,* said, "I wish God wouldn't put so many disguises on His blessings."

But He doesn't! We do it! We disguise His blessings.

Christ's death on the cross was a blessing, but His disciples looked upon it only as a horrible act of injustice. Christ's ascension into Heaven was a blessing, but it was viewed by His disciples as a time of loneliness and fear for those who were left behind. The establishing of the church was a blessing, too, but the Jews saw it as a monumental threat to their relationship with God.

God gives only blessings! Man, however, puts on all manner of disguises that frequently keep him from recognizing them as blessings.

The Communion service is one of God's special blessings to us. Don't let the disguises of habit, ritual, or sentimentality rob you of its meaning. See it as a blessing without disguise!

Prayer
Father, open our eyes to see things as they are. Help us not to distort what is beautiful or cover up what you want revealed for all to see. For Jesus' sake, amen.

Picture Perfect

Scripture Reading: 1 Peter 1:8, 9

An old expression says, "One picture is worth a thousand words."

The Lord's Supper is a picture. Paul wrote, "As often as ye eat this bread, and drink this cup, ye do show the Lord's death till he come."

The Lord's Supper, then, is a kind of picture portrait.

How many words could you write about it if you had to? Could you write at least a thousand words? I hope that what the Lord's Supper portrays has not become so commonplace that it no longer speaks words of comfort and inspiration to you.

Every worthwhile picture is worth at least a thousand words. If the right words do not come through to us in this service, perhaps it is not the fault of the picture but of the spirit of those who behold it. Much of the beauty, indeed, is in the eyes of the beholder.

Prayer

Open our eyes and give us a fresh glimpse of You, O Lord! Help us to see the beauty that has caused men and women for centuries to speak words of praise, courage, and faith. Help our words to be worthy of Him who is being portrayed in this holy celebration. In Jesus' name, amen.

The Passover Meal

Scripture Reading: Colossians 2:16, 17

The feast of the Passover was among the most important of all the religious observances of the Jewish year. This observance reminded the Jews of the time when "death" passed over them in Egypt and slew the firstborn of every Egyptian family. The wine reminded them of the lamb's blood that they sprinkled on their doorposts to save themselves. The unleavened bread was a reminder of God and His purity. The dish of bitter herbs reminded them of the bitter and cruel experiences they suffered at the hands of the Egyptians.

Before the Passover feast was eaten, their houses were thoroughly swept and cleaned. Every dish and cooking utensil was washed. All the spices and impurities were removed from the house so only the memorial items were present.

It was at the observance of this Passover feast that Jesus instituted the Lord's Supper. For us, too, this should be a time of housecleaning, a time when the impurities in our hearts are removed and the purity of God is remembered. We should take thought, too, of the bitterness of a world that hasn't yet taken the time to know Him.

However, in the observance of the Lord's Supper there is a crucial difference from the Passover feast. Here at the Lord's table our sins are not merely passed over; they are washed away! This is not a picture of a covering but of a cleansing!

Prayer

Father, sweep our hearts clean from thoughts we shouldn't have. Wash thoroughly our motives for worship today, so that we all can stand before You as newborn children waiting for wonderful things to happen. Create in us a pure heart! In Jesus' name, amen.

The Light That's Right

Scripture Reading: Romans 12:1, 2

Most of us have read the story in the Bible of the ten virgins. Five were said to be wise and five were called foolish. They were called foolish not because they had done anything terribly wrong, but because they had done the right thing foolishly.

All had been given lamps and oil to burn in them, and told to be ready when the bridegroom came. The first five took an extra supply of oil with them, while the foolish maidens took only the supply of oil contained within the lamps themselves. As the lamps burned throughout the night, the supply of oil in the lamps was depleted. Those without any reserve oil had to return to the village for more. Then the bridegroom came during their absence, and their opportunity to see him was lost.

The apostle's admonition not to forsake "the assembling of ourselves together" is sound advice for those who need their faith reserves replenished. The discipline of regular worship helps us to trim our wicks so that we might reflect more light than heat and more fire than smoke in our faith.

The Lord's Supper is a reminder to all that while we are only human vessels, limited in our capacity to brighten the darkness around us, God's capacity is unlimited. Here at the Lord's table we are urged to remember Him who said, "I am the light of the world."

Prayer

Our heavenly Father, we confess that we are all still a little afraid of the darkness. We also confess that we are the ones who have created most of the darkness we have had to live with. Keep us from following lesser lights. Keep our eyes on Jesus. In His name, amen.

A Scandalous Messiah

Scripture Reading: John 8:31, 32, 36

We have all, in the course of our lifetimes, set a trap for someone or something. The Greeks called a trap a *scandalon*. It is from this word that the English word "scandal" is derived. In Jesus' day there were many kinds of traps or *scandalons*. Sometimes a rock was used as a *scandalon* to trip or trap people while they journeyed in the darkness.

Jesus was once referred to as a scandal! He was a rock in man's way that made many men stumble. People still stumble over Him today. The Jews in His day stubbornly rejected Him as the Messiah. Their scandalous behavior showed who had really tripped up and become trapped.

Placed in every man's pathway is the rock upon which God built His church, Jesus Christ. He represents salvation to those who accept Him, and ruin to those who do not. This time of

Communion is an opportunity to erase any scandal in your life by accepting Him who was willing to become a scandal for us. If one must be trapped in life, let it be by God's truth, which will fully "set you free."

Prayer

Our Father, help us to know that we are never quite as free as we are when we have made peace with You. Thank You for picking us up when we have stumbled badly. Help us not to become trapped by our own conceit. In Jesus' name, amen.

Being Fashionable

Scripture Reading: Ephesians 6:13-18

The first hint of sacrifice in the Bible occurs in the third chapter of Genesis, where it mentions that God made clothing for Adam and Eve out of animal skins. An animal had to be slain so man's body could be covered.

The last sacrifice we read of in the Bible was that of Jesus Christ. Here again, the innocent had to die for the guilty, this time to cover man's spiritual body. Even the apostle Paul speaks of "putting on Christ" as if He were a type of garment we must wear.

If you are style conscious, it is important to know that the Christian faith will always be fashionable. It will always cover your needs and give you full protection.

We gather around the table of the Lord to remember our great Designer, who will not only clothe us with righteousness but with immortality as well!

Prayer

We confess that our own righteousness is as rags compared to Your divine beauty. Keep us from following beliefs and ideas that seem stylish for a while but fade in their glory. Give us a look of eternity, so we will always be fashionable with You. In Jesus' name, amen.

The High Cost of Selling Out

Scripture Reading: Matthew 26:14-16

"Then one of the twelve, called Judas Iscariot, went unto the chief priests, and said unto them, What will ye give me, and I will deliver him unto you? And they covenanted with him for thirty pieces of silver."

Every man has his price. Most of us, in the idealism of our youth, protest that we have no price. But as opportunity passes us by again and again in life, sometimes a person offers us the right price for our soul—and we take it!

The actions of Judas Iscariot are an accurate reflection of our own behavior when we sell out to the other side. We can do this by compromising the truth, or by being too timid in the expression of our faith. We can do it by easing off in the discipline of church attendance, Christian stewardship, Bible study, and prayer.

We do not have to sell Jesus for money to be guilty of selling Him out. When we sell our souls, the price is never right.

Prayer

Dear Lord, we are not very happy about the many ways we have compromised our faith and commitment to You. It is not even consoling to us that no one else has noticed. We notice! This knowledge of our own lack of dedication troubles us. Firm up within us a new desire to pay the price of Christian discipleship. Amen.

The Beginning and the End

Scripture Reading: John 10:10

The apostle Paul tells us that the gospel is summarized in the death, burial, and resurrection of Jesus Christ. His burial is pictured to us in the ordinance of baptism. We are reminded of His resurrection by the fact that we worship on Sunday, the day He arose from the grave. The Lord's Supper reminds us of His death; the pouring of His blood and the giving of His body for our redemption.

We remember His death as often as we do His resurrection—fifty-two times a year. This is as it should be. The Lord's Supper is as important to us as Sunday worship. The Lord's Supper proclaims, "He died." Sunday worship proclaims, "He lives." Christ's death, as celebrated through the Lord's Supper, is the beginning of God's love story to man; Christ's resurrection, as celebrated through Sunday worship, is the exciting conclusion.

Three thousand years ago Job asked the question, "If a man die, shall he live again?" The Lord's Supper reminds us of the Son of Man, who died; Sunday worship reminds us that He lives again. And so can we!

Prayer

Father, help us to remember that what sometimes seems to be the end for us is not an end, but only a bridge to a new beginning. Give us the courage to cross over and start again. Amen.

Heavenly Music

Scripture Reading: Psalm 98:4-9

Most record players today will operate at three or four different speeds. The speed you select does not depend on the tune you wish to hear, but rather on the number of revolutions per minute the master disc was turning when the tune was recorded. Nor does the speed at which it was recorded govern the tempo or the volume reproduced.

All of us here this morning will probably express our faith at different speeds and on different emotional levels. Some may be wildly enthusiastic while others will be quiet and reserved. However, the melody we all seek to play by our sincere worship is one that tells of God's love for us. This melody can be played at all speeds. It can be played by children, teenagers, newlyweds, mothers, dads, successful people, ordinary people, and even those who feel they have failed in life. Each must find his own speed, and then try to be the finest instrument he can be for channeling this beautiful melody.

The Communion service is one of those times when we experience this melody most clearly and forcefully. We must listen well in these next few moments. What we play back to the world must have the highest fidelity possible, and not the usual distortions of lesser melodies.

Prayer

Our Father in Heaven, keep our melodies sweet. Keep our voices from becoming strident and harsh. Make our church family hum with the kind of harmony that will make even the angels listen. We know we are still unfinished symphonies. In Jesus' name, amen.

> "And when the Chief Shepherd appears, you will receive the crown of glory that will never fade away."

Shepherding Away My Wants

Scripture Reading: 1 Peter 5:4

The Lord is my shepherd, and even though I feel I need many things, I know I shall never want for anything that God knows I really need.

He makes me to lie down in peace even when the world is shouting, "There is no peace!" He leads me beside the still waters of faith in God and love for others.

When I feel that all is lost, He restores my soul. He leads me in the paths of righteousness, not because it is the safe place to walk, or even the respected path, but it is where God is, and I know He wants me for His company.

Yea, though I walk through valleys where death frightens me at every turn, I will not be frightened because I know that You, God, are right behind me, holding me up all the way!

I know that You have prepared a far better table for me than have my enemies. In fact, You have treated me like a king compared to what the world has offered me.

But this one thing I know: whatever comes, I am ready for it. I know that it will be for my own good and that Your mercy is far greater than my obedience. As far as I am concerned, eternal life for me has already begun.

Prayer

Father, it is much easier to pray courageously than to be courageous! Bind our prayers more closely to our deeds, we pray. Amen.

Customs, Culture, and Communion

Scripture Reading: Hebrews 10:23-25

The apostle Paul would probably feel a little out of place in our worship service.

Paul often worshiped very early or very late in the day, for many of the Christians were slaves and worked long hours. We worship in the middle of the day. Their services were probably informal. Each might bring a hymn to church of his or her own choice, knowing that it might be one of many selected for the worship program. Our worship services today are usually planned in advance and run smoothly without interruptions from the congregation from start to finish. The leader of the service in Paul's day was called the president; the one who presided. Today the leader is usually referred to as the minister. In Paul's day, the church met in secrecy. Their numbers were few. Only Christians attended. Today, the size of our congregation is large. We meet in the open, and often there are as many outsiders present as there are members.

This may sound as if we have departed from the ways of God. But in truth we still meet for the same reasons God's people have always met, and with the same spirit of need and faith as did our early brothers and sisters.

In Paul's time, a meal was often arranged for all to eat together. The Lord's Supper was eaten following this meal. We have no meal to serve with the Lord's Supper, but we do offer these emblems in the same spirit as did the early Christians. We urge you to remember the same admonition Jesus gave the people in His day: "This do in remembrance of me."

Prayer

Father, some things are different today in the way we worship You. We hope these differences do not displease You. We would much rather be out of step with the times than to be out of step with You! In Jesus' name, amen.

Communion and Union

Scripture Reading: 1 Corinthians 10:16, 17

Sadly, the Communion service has been the subject of much division! Some feel that all who partake should drink from a common cup. Others feel that individual cups are preferable. Some churches use fermented wine while others would be deeply offended with such a practice. Some churches even use water! Some churches commune spiritually and use no physical emblems at all. Some churches observe the Lord's Supper every week while others do it monthly, quarterly, or yearly. Some say the very presence of Christ's body is experienced in the Communion service while others say it is less mystical and more memorial in nature.

We do not seek to define all that the Lord's Supper is, for to define it would be to limit it. We simply say, "This is the Lord's Supper." It is not our supper! It is a time of Communion with Him. It is not just a Communion with one another. This experience can be as great or as insignificant as we wish to make it.

The closer one stands to the light the bigger the shadow one casts. This service reminds us of "the light of the world." Our stature is increased when we are shone upon by the "sun of righteousness."

Prayer

Father, add to our wavering faith a more complete trust. Subtract pettiness from our spirit. Multiply our effectiveness by making each of us willing ministers of the higher way. Divide the opportunities for doing good things equally among us all so that even the least of Your children will feel an important part in Your kingdom's growth! Amen.

Unity in Diversity

Scripture Reading: 1 John 17:20, 21

A great deal has been said about Christian unity. Some people have confused unity with conformity and uniformity. Some would like to make all Christians alike with few differences among them.

No two branches on a tree are exactly alike,

yet there is unity in all the branches of a tree because they are all attached to the same trunk. Personal differences of opinion will occur in the church, and we should not seriously worry when these differences arise.

The table of Christ is the one place where all Christians should stand in perfect unity in humble remembrance of the Christ! It is from this place that we all must begin marching off from the same left foot, in hope that our unity of spirit will prevail amid the inevitable diversity of actions and opinions.

Prayer

We know, our heavenly Father, that there is no discord in You. We know, too, that You know Your entire family on earth by name, even though we are ignorant of many of our brothers and sisters. Help us, in this Communion service, to see You more clearly so that we will be able to recognize our larger Christian family more easily. Amen.

Physical Acts and Spiritual Visions

Scripture Reading: 1 Corinthians 10:1-4

People sometimes wonder why it is that the church, being a spiritual institution, places such an emphasis on physical acts and physical objects used in worship. Baptism is a physical act. The money that is collected is a physical object. The church building is physical. The Christ we worship was a physical person.

However, the physical is only a vehicle for the spiritual. The meaning lies not in what you see and witness in the church service; rather, what you witness in the church service helps you see more deeply the meaning of a truly spiritual life. The beauty is not in the offering you put in the plate, but in you as an offering person. All of that which you see and hear is a means to a spiritual end, not merely an end in itself!

The Son of God came so that men could see

Him as the Christ. Some, however, see Him only as Jesus of Nazareth. In the emblems of the Communion service, some see merely the unleavened bread and the fruit of the vine. Others see the purity of Christ's life and the supreme sacrifice He made for us. Those who are wise learn that there is much more to life than meets the eye. The Lord's Supper is for the wise.

Prayer

Our Father, help us to see clearly the beautiful meaning hidden in the symbols of this holy Communion service. In Jesus' name, amen.

Reasons for Worship

Scripture Reading: 1 Corinthians 11:23-26

People come to worship for many reasons. Some of the reasons are noble and praiseworthy; some are not.

Some people come to impress others. It usually doesn't take much to impress most people—a new car, a new suit, an improved handicap in golf. People who are having deep and personal troubles, though, are not easily impressed by such things. Someone else's new car can never quite take away a person's hurt.

Some come to worship because they feel guilty about things. While worship can bring some feeling of relief, that relief usually lasts for a very short time. It takes much more than ritual worship to dispel our guilt.

Some are forced to come! Just as we can prime a well, we can prime a little interest from others in the church from time to time. But we cannot irrigate a field with prime water only. A well must have water in it before we can bring any water up, no matter how hard we prime it. Church services have their greatest blessings for those who dip from their own springs of motivation and desire.

Some come to church services because it's good for business. While church attendance probably is good for business, it is much better for businessmen and businesswomen!

There are all kinds of reasons why family members still gather around the family table even though they could all have scattered to other eating places. There comes a time, however, when the loving father says, "Let's stop talking and let's eat!"

Prayer

Father, we are here today for many reasons. We realize that some of these reasons may not be very good ones. In spite of whatever has prompted us to come, give us such a great blessing that we'll never want to stay away again. In Jesus' name, amen.

The Body of Christ

Scripture Reading: 1 Corinthians 12:12-14

I don't suppose it surprises you when you hear the minister say, "The church is the body of Christ." But when the apostle Paul said that for the first time, people were amazed, startled, and shocked!

But Paul went one step further. He said that Christians are all "membranes" of the body of Christ. Never before had anyone conceived of being such an intimate part of someone else's body, until Paul described us as being a part of Christ's body.

The Bible never speaks of us as members of Christ's church, but as members of His body. Christ did not die to invite you to a church. He died to invite you to himself. We don't need more church buildings to put Christians in; we need more Christians in the body.

The Lord's Supper reminds us that just as this loaf and cup become a part of our physical bodies, so are we a part of Christ's spiritual body. It is a comforting thought to know that the world will never again be able to find a tomb large enough to contain Christ's body.

Prayer

Our heavenly Father, it is good to know that we are not alone. It is good to feel an intimate attachment to all who eat and drink these emblems at this table. Help us to feel the same dependence on one another that the parts of our bodies have for one another. Keep us from crippling the body of Christ by any unkindness toward another member. In Jesus' name, amen.

Loudly Cries the Silence

Scripture Reading: Psalm 46:10

The word "communion" is very much like the word "communicate." This is what the Communion service attempts to accomplish—to communicate. There is a message in this simple act of worship around the Lord's table.

This is perhaps the quietest time in our worship service, but the message is the loudest. We hope it is so loud that you can't hear yourself think. We hope you can only hear God's thinking.

However, good communication involves more than volume. We hope this Communion time speaks *clearly* to you as well. We hope that it speaks more to you than mere habit, custom, ritual, or doctrine. This act of worship around the table seeks to communicate a message. It seeks to communicate a "presence." It is not merely a time to feel something, but to feel Someone.

As the Greeks said to the disciple Philip, "We would see Jesus." We cannot serve Him to you on so many plates, but we can ask you to serve Him, to feel His presence in your life, to hear and recognize His thoughts mingling with your own. This is called "communication." It is also called "Communion."

Prayer

Father, we are listening for words that cannot be heard with the ears. We are looking for a presence that cannot be seen with the eyes. We are looking to touch what we know we cannot feel with our fingers. Our longings at this moment are beyond the reach of our senses, and yet, we know with full faith that we will hear, we will see, and we will feel Your special nearness in this Communion service! In Jesus' name, amen.

God, Our Reservoir

Scripture Reading: Ephesians 3:14-19

Lawrence of Arabia brought several native chieftains with him to the Paris Peace Conference years ago. Those desert leaders were amazed at many things, but nothing astonished them as much as the running water in their hotel rooms. They knew the scarcity and value of water, yet here it was to be had, free and inexhaustible, by the simple turning of a faucet's handle.

When they were preparing to leave Paris, Lawrence found them trying to take the faucets with them so that in the desert they could have water whenever they desired it. He tried to explain that behind these faucets were huge reservoirs and that without this abundant supply the faucets were useless. But it was easier for the chieftains to believe that the faucets were magic.

Some people think of the Communion emblems as representing a kind of magical faucet. They see within the loaf and cup certain powerful qualities that will produce life-changing results in the person who consumes them. But, like the faucet, it is that which stands behind these emblems that gives them power and meaning. It is not we who turn the power on when we partake, but the power of God that turns us on when we break bread together. And while we cannot pack this power up and take it with us wherever we go, God can hold us in His possession wherever we go. Whenever we need to draw on power beyond our own, God's reservoir is sufficient to supply our every need.

Prayer

Father, we have been turned on by many things. We have also tried to turn others on by our own charm, talents, and clever devices. But we confess our powerlessness this morning. Like so often before, many of us have simply run dry. It is discouraging to draw from an empty well! Give us a clear vision of our true source of power. Deliver us from substitutes that only promise but never provide the lasting satisfaction we all long for. In Jesus' name, amen.

Give and Take

Scripture Reading: 1 Corinthians 10:13
(New English Bible)

"The Lord gave, and the Lord hath taken away; blessed be the name of the Lord."

Do you know when that statement was first made? One thousand years ago? Two thousand? Three thousand years ago? No, even further back in time than that. Most of us are still trying to develop the kind of trusting faith shown by that person in his statement.

God never removes anything from anyone without giving that person something in return to fill its place. He used the flood waters to destroy the world, but He started a new and better world through the righteous family of Noah. Later God took away political freedom from the Jewish nation, but He gave them a new and better King, the Messiah He had promised them. The body of this Messiah was taken and drained of its life-giving blood, but God gave us this Communion loaf and cup to help us remember that King of kings. The plan and design of God has always been one of giving and taking!

We must be tuned in to the divine plan of "give and take." When someone we love or something we value deeply is removed from our presence, we should remember God's give-and-take design. What we see as "taking" may actually be a picture of "giving." He may be giving us the opportunity to exercise and affirm our faith and trust in Him. This kind of faith can never be taken away.

This quiet time around the table of the Lord is not a replacement for that which you think has been taken from you this past week. It is an opportunity for you to see the gift that God has for you. Only those who can say, "Blessed be the name of the Lord," can find it!

Prayer

Father, help us to see that losses are not always losses, and gains are not always gains. At this table this morning, remind us again that what looks like the end can really be a great beginning for us. In Jesus' name, amen.

The Outside of the Cup

Luke 11:37-40
(New English Bible)

"When Jesus had finished speaking, a Pharisee invited him to a meal. Jesus came in and sat down. The Pharisee noticed with surprise that Jesus had not begun by washing before the meal. But the Lord said to him: "You Pharisees! You clean the outside of cup and plate; but inside you there is nothing but greed and wickedness. You fools! Did not he who made the outside make the inside too?"

Dirty hands were less important to Jesus than were clean thoughts. Outward appearances, like the outside of a cup or a robed Pharisee in the temple, did not impress Him or move Him to great admiration. But He was moved when He saw inner cleanness. He saw it in the heart of a repentant woman whose past had been unrighteous. He saw it in the publican who sorrowed because he was such a terrible sinner. He saw it in the lives of little children who could have been turned inside out and found to be clean on both sides.

We have gathered together in this worship service not to clean the outer but the inner person. You and I will not be judged by what we take into our mouths, but by that which comes out of them. We can easily cleanse the outer person by allowing our lives to be moved by the ritual and aesthetic overtones of this Communion service. Yet if this is all the Lord's Supper means to us, we are no better off than the man who washes his fork and then proceeds to eat with his fingers!

We introduce you to the Lamb of God, who cleanses the inner places where true health really begins.

Prayer

Father, we come today with many blemishes in our lives. We don't want to take them home with us. We have come here for a cleansing. We may not go home wiser or more courageous, but we must go home clean. Cleanse us so that the weight of our wrongs does not burden us unto death! In Jesus' name, amen.

Life Comes From Death

Scripture Reading: Matthew 10:39

Jesus told a parable about a sower who cast some seed on the ground. In that parable Jesus said that a grain must first fall to the ground and die and be buried before life can come from it.

Watchman Nee, the great Chinese Christian preacher, expanded on the story in a sermon once. Even though the seed is alive, he said, it must break through the outer husk or kernel of the grain. Until the break is made in the covering, the seed cannot grow.

We Christians possess a powerful life force within us, but it cannot grow and be seen while it remains bound and leashed within us. Our task, therefore, is not one of searching for the abundant life in the world around us, but to recognize and release that abundant life within us. Jesus will not break through our shell. It must be broken from within. Once we do it we will discover how much life can be gained by letting loose our lives for God!

Prayer

Our Father, we sense that the saints were right when they said that it is only the surrendered life that is worth living! We are reluctant to let go of our self-centered personalities and ambitions, but we also know that there will be no true life for us unless we can destroy the old cravings. Help us to die a little in this service so we can live a life of greater service. Amen.

The Old Rugged Cross

(Hymn 317)

Scripture Reading: Galatians 6:14

George Bennard testifies;
"I love that old rugged cross."

It "has a wondrous attraction for me."

"To the old rugged cross I will ever be true."

"I'll cherish the old rugged cross."

What a strange way to speak of an instrument of execution! To get the feeling of how unlovely an object the cross was in Jesus' time, we can substitute in Mr. Bennard's phrases the names of more modern means of execution:

"I love that old firing squad."

"The gallows has a wondrous attraction for me."

"To the gas chamber I will ever be true."

"I'll cherish the electric chair."

In an era when the cross has become a decorative object and even a good-luck charm, we need the reminder that originally it was ugly and monstrous, and it became a thing of beauty only because "twas on that old cross Jesus suffered and died, to pardon and sanctify me."

As we prepare to share in these emblems that point us to the old rugged cross, let us see that cross as it was: a cruel, shameful, brutal instrument of torture. But let us also reflect on how Jesus has transformed it into a symbol of love, mercy, and hope.

Prayer
Our Father, help us to see past the sentimental aura that often surrounds the cross and behold the bleeding, brutalized Savior who hung there. In Jesus' name, amen.

I Love Him Because He First Loved Me

(Hymn 214)

Scripture Reading: 1 John 4:7-10, 19

Who is going to take the initiative? That question comes up in many of our human relationships. We might have an argument with a member of our family or a fellow church member. It is time to apologize to one another, but our pride prevents our speaking first. If only that other person would take the initiative, the problem would be solved.

Frank E. Roush reminds us in this hymn that in man's relationship with God, it was God who took the initiative. Because we chose to live according to our sinful desires, an argument existed between us and God. Frustrated and miserable, we longed for a way to straighten things out, but we were too proud to take the first step. And then we learned to our amazement that our loving heavenly Father had already taken the initiative. By sending His Son to earth to die for us, He provided the means of dissolving the sin barrier between Him and man.

And now we gather around the Lord's table as one way of demonstrating that "we love Him because He first loved us." Let us share in the emblems of His love, and let us love Him in return.

Prayer

Our Father, open our eyes to the greatness of Your love for us. Help us to be reflectors of that love. In Jesus' name, amen.

Rock of Ages

(Hymn 243)

Scripture Reading: 2 Corinthians 7:9, 10

Have you ever shed a tear at Communion time? It is desirable that you should become emotionally involved in this act of worship, but consider Augustus M. Toplady's prayer in stanza two: "Could my tears forever flow, all for sin could not atone; Thou must save, and Thou alone."

As children we learned that at times we could soften the stern countenances of offended parents and escape the consequences of our misdeeds by resorting to tears. Surely, we reason, God is even more sympathetic and understanding than our parents. Our weeping, our groaning over our errors should convince Him to pardon us.

Beware of the idea that expressions of sorrow over sin somehow justify us before God. Remember the striking words of the Lord in Joel 2:13: "Rend your heart, and not your garments, and turn unto the Lord your God." The people of Judah were accustomed to tearing their clothing as an outward token of sorrow, but God demanded a profound inner change that would lead to reformation of life. In the same way God is looking beyond our easy tears, our sentimental weeping, and urging us to say in our hearts, "Lord, change me! Help me to change the way I think, speak, and act!"

So do not restrain the tears if they tend to come during the Lord's Supper. But recognize that tears alone do not constitute repentance before God. Come before Him with prayer of surrender. Tell Him, *"Thou must save, and Thou alone."* And then trust Him to cleanse you from sin and keep your feet firmly planted on the rock of salvation.

Prayer

Our gracious Father, help us to make this Communion a time of thorough repentance. In Jesus' name, amen.

Ivory Palaces

(Hymn 375)

Scripture Reading: 2 Corinthians 8:9; 9:15

One of the delights of reading the Old Testament lies in coming across phrases or terms that have become familiar through the singing of hymns. The description of the majesty and power of a king in Psalm 45, for example, is quite applicable to our King, Jesus Christ. Then we come to verse eight: "All thy garments smell of myrrh, and aloes, and cassia, out of the ivory palaces, whereby they have made thee glad."

This verse supplied the inspiration for Henry Barraclough's hymn, "Ivory Palaces." Mr. Barraclough interpreted the ivory palaces of Psalm 45:8 in terms of Paul's great New Testament statement: "For ye know the grace of our Lord Jesus Christ, that, though he was rich, yet for your sakes he became poor, that ye through his poverty might be rich" (2 Corinthians 8:9).

Here we must utilize our imagination. What was it like for Jesus Christ to forsake Heaven's splendors in order to live the humble life of a carpenter on earth? How much of a sacrifice was it for the Son of God to suffer separation from His Father for a time? What did it mean for the Creator of man to undergo brutal, painful treatment and finally death at the hands of His creatures? What a thrilling thought it is that the King of the universe so lived among us!

And how fitting it is that He left such a simple memorial by which we can remember each week His sacrifice for us. He who came forth from the ivory palaces might well have chosen to be remembered by the richest and most elaborate of feasts. But He selected instead this humble bread and fruit of the vine as the symbols of His suffering for us.

Prayer

Gracious heavenly Father, thank You for the gift of Your Son. May the wonder of this truth fill our minds and hearts as we partake. In Jesus' name, amen.

O Sacred Head, Now Wounded

(Hymn 338)

Scripture Reading: Revelation 5:11, 12

This hymn of German authorship asks a remarkable question in stanza four:

> What language shall I borrow
> To thank thee, dearest Friend,
> For this thy dying sorrow,
> Thy mercy without end?

To be so caught up in a spirit of thanksgiving that our native tongue would be inadequate to express what we feel—that is the experience to which these words point us. But for many of us who have been Christians a long time, the spirit of wonder regarding the cross has diminished. Perhaps it is a case of familiarity dulling our senses—we have heard so many times and in so many ways of Jesus' sacrifice for us, that it simply does not stir our emotions as it once did.

And yet, is this not one benefit of regular communing around the Lord's table, that we be so powerfully reminded of what happened at Calvary as to stir our entire beings? These emblems speak of our sins—sins that were an offense to the God who made us and loved us. These emblems testify to God's judgment against sin, for they represent the suffering and death that is "the wages of sin" (Romans 6:23). These emblems portray Jesus Christ's terrible combat with sin and death at Calvary. These emblems are reminders of resurrection morning, when Satan's hold on sinful man was shattered by the risen Christ.

How can a story like that ever become dull? How can a salvation such as we enjoy ever lose its sense of wonder? Let us not permit the hectic busyness of our affairs, the attractions and distractions of a heathen society, or the tendency to distort our faith into a repetitious ritual deprive us of a joyous thanksgiving at the Lord's table.

"What language shall I borrow?" the hymn writer asks. We need not worry about the language of our lips if the language of our hearts is that of grateful praise.

Prayer

Heavenly Father, enable us to experience that inexpressible wonder and joy that Christ's death on the cross should bring us. In His name, amen.

It Is Well With My Soul
(Hymn 73)

Scripture Reading: 1 Corinthians 6:9-11

Have you ever been so overwhelmed at receiving a gift or favor that you could respond only with an outpouring of appreciation and praise? This appears to have been the experience of Horatio Spafford in this hymn. Consider these awe-inspired words:

> My sin—oh the bliss of this glorious tho't—
> My sin—not in part, but the whole,
> Is nailed to the cross, and I bear it no more,
> Praise the Lord, praise the Lord, O my soul!

We can share Mr. Spafford's sense of awe when we think that *all* our sin, not just part of it, was nailed to Jesus' cross.

Many of our sins seem to us quite forgiveable. A slip of the tongue, an unguarded thought, a hasty act—surely God will forgive these. So we reason. But what about those big, ugly sins that we committed, realizing at the time that we were disobeying God's will? How can God release us from guilt for our deliberate lies, our unrestrained flights into covetousness, our premeditated acts of vengeance on those who did us some real or imagined wrong? Is it not too much to expect that God would blot out such a record as that?

Paul gives a detailed list of some of these big, ugly sins. "Be not deceived: neither fornicators, nor idolators, nor adulterers, nor effeminate, nor abusers of themselves with mankind, nor thieves, nor covetous, nor drunkards, nor revilers, nor extortioners, shall inherit the kingdom of God."

That sounds pretty dismal for all of us big sinners, doesn't it? But notice what Paul says in the next verse: "And such were some of you: but ye are washed, but ye are sanctified, but ye are justified in the name of the Lord Jesus, and by the Spirit of our God."

Prayer

Our Father, whether our sins are big or little, earthshaking or insignificant, You have nailed them all to the cross of Calvary. Help each one of us to understand this, and to rejoice in that knowledge with praise and thanksgiving. In Jesus' name, amen.

All That Thrills My Soul

(Hymn 65)

Scripture Reading: Romans 11:33-36

Have you ever seen the diagram that illustrates the relationship between feelings, facts, and faith? It pictures a train with three cars. The car or engine labeled "facts" comes first, followed by "faith," with the "feelings" car coming last. This indicates that the proper sequence in Christian experience is learning the facts as they are revealed in the Bible, responding to these facts by faith, and only then enjoying the feelings of joy, peace, etc.

People often confuse the role of feelings. They may question the Scriptural plan of salvation because they *felt* they were saved before they repented or were baptized. Or they may substitute feelings for actual reasoned faith in the Christ of the Bible.

Because of this confusion, preachers and teachers sometimes tend to disparage feelings, but that is also an error. Christianity is not a cold, logical, mechanical kind of life. When Thoro Harris testifies, "All that thrills my soul is Jesus," he is echoing the excitement of the book of Acts, in which we read of Christianity that was characterized by a warmth of feeling and an eager readiness to share a thrilling gospel message.

Certainly the Lord's Supper is not meant to be a formal, mechanical observance. We should come to our time of communing in this spirit:

What a wonderful redemption!
   Never can a mortal know
How my sin, tho' red like crimson
   Can be whiter than the snow.

Let us fix our minds firmly once again on this fact: Jesus Christ has died to free us from the curse of sin. Let us reaffirm our faith in Christ and in His redeeming blood. And then let us give ourselves to those soul-thrilling feelings that are a natural response to that wonderful redemption.

Prayer

Heavenly Father, give us relief from formal, lifeless worship. Help us to experience the excitement of the gospel as those first Christians did. In Jesus' name, amen.

Amazing Grace

(Hymn 487)

Scripture Reading: Ephesians 2:4-10

John Newton, author of "Amazing Grace," left the following epitaph:

> John Newton, clerk
> Once an infidel and libertine,

> A servant of slaves in Africa,
> Was, by the rich mercy
> of our Lord and Saviour,
> Jesus Christ,
> Preserved, restored, pardoned,
> And appointed to preach the faith
> He had long labored to destroy. . . .

When Mr. Newton spoke of "a wretch like me," of being lost and blind, it was not mere poetic effect, but a genuine description of a life that grace transformed.

But few of us are acquainted with the life of John Newton. This hymn probably appeals to us more because it speaks accurately of our own spiritual experience. While few of us were "notorious sinners," each of us is aware of the wretchedness our open sins and our hidden sins bring to our hearts.

And so it is indeed *amazing* grace that we celebrate in the Lord's Supper. As we await the emblems, we can meditate on the wonder of it, the inexpressible marvel of it, that God in His grace sent Jesus Christ to die for us.

But grace looks not only to the past:

Thro' many dangers, toils, and snares,
I have already come;
'Tis grace that bro't me safe thus far
And grace will lead me home.

What a glorious thought this is! "By grace are ye saved through faith; and that not of yourselves: it is the gift of God" (Ephesians 2:8). And this grace operated not only at the time we were baptized; it continues to surround us as we struggle to live for Christ in a wicked world.

Oh, yes—"Amazing grace! how *sweet* the sound!" Let us now enjoy that sweetness.

Prayer

Dear Father, help us to perceive the richness and the fullness of that great New Testament doctrine of grace. In Jesus' name, amen.

Lead Me to Calvary

(Hymn 337)

Scripture Reading: 1 Peter 2:21-25

It is amazing what human beings are capable of forgetting. Politicians forget their campaign promises. Husbands have difficulty recalling the dates of their wedding anniversaries. Children struggle to remember to perform simple household duties.

Jennie E. Hussey reminds us that we are prone to forget even spiritual benefits:

> Lest I forget Gethsemane;
> Lest I forget Thine agony;
> Lest I forget Thy love for me,
> Lead me to Calvary.

Jesus provided the Lord's Supper as a regular reminder of what He has done for us. How can we forget when we permit the broken bread to remind us of the agonies His body endured for us? How can we fail to think of His love when we hold the cup and see in its crimson contents the blood shed for us?

Of course it is possible to miss the spiritual benefits of the Lord's Supper. We can partake of these emblems in a thoughtless manner. When Communion time arrives we must be ready to be led to Calvary. Only then can our very human tendency to forget be reversed. And then we can echo the psalmist's cry: "Bless the Lord, O my soul, and forget not all his benefits" (Psalm 103:2).

Prayer

Dear heavenly Father, forgive us our forgetfulness! Remind us vividly of the upper room, the cross, and the empty tomb. In Jesus' name, amen.

Cleanse Me

(Hymn 252)

Scripture Reading: 1 John 1:5-10

The words of the first stanza of this hymn by J. Edwin Orr are about as close to Scripture as a hymn can be. They reflect the last two verses of Psalm 139: "Search me, O God, and know my heart: try me, and know my thoughts: and see if there be any wicked way in me, and lead me in the way everlasting."

David's purpose here seems a matter of protesting his innocence, his purity, rather than confessing his sin. But we do not violate the Scriptural meaning when we use this prayer, as Mr. Orr does, to acknowledge our innermost sins and to seek God's cleansing for them.

God knows us intimately. We may tend to think that an impure thought or an unworthy motive escapes His gaze, but the Scripture teaches otherwise: "All things are naked and opened unto the eyes of him with whom we have to do" (Hebrews 4:13). Why, then, does He require us to confess those hidden sins? The answer is that He wants us to trust Him enough to be open before Him. He wants us to surrender ourselves so completely to Him that we will place our lives entirely in the focus of His searching gaze.

The Communion hour bids us to come in the spirit of Psalm 139. If we have withheld from God's presence some part of our secret selves, now is the moment to release our grip upon it. If we have regarded iniquity in our hearts (Psalm 66:18), this is the time to confess it and forsake it. Only then can we experience the blessedness of the promise of 1 John 1:9: "If we confess our sins, he is faithful and just to forgive us our sins, and to cleanse us from all unrighteousness."

Prayer

Great God and Father, You know all about us. Lead us to be open and honest before You. In Jesus' name, amen.

Tell Me the Old, Old Story

(Hymn 79)

Scripture Reading: 1 Timothy 1:15

Catherine Hankey's request is also ours: "Tell me the story slowly, that I may take it in—that wonderful redemption, God's remedy for sin." Perhaps we should never partake of the Lord's Supper without a simple, unhurried recounting of the basic facts of the gospel. Let the story sink again into your minds and hearts:

God created you and set His love upon you.... You broke God's laws and turned your back on His love.... And then you learned that His love was so great that He had sent His Son to earth to die for you.... On the cross that stood on Calvary Jesus endured incredible agony and humiliation—for you. . . . On the cross Jesus underwent the dark experience of death—for you. . . . And for you, that you may have a fresh opportunity to enjoy God's extended gift of love, Jesus burst forth from the tomb. What a wonderful "old, old story" we are remembering!

Why do we have difficulty in making this old, old story a personal matter? Perhaps we feel that it is too good to be true in our lives—we are not deserving enough; we are not really worth all that trouble. How we need to lay hold on the amazing realization Catherine Hankey expressed when she wrote, "Tell me the story softly, with earnest tones and grave; remember *I'm* the sinner whom Jesus came to save." The apostle Paul put it this way: "This is a faithful saying, and worthy of all acceptation, that Christ Jesus came into the world to save sinners; of whom I am chief" (1 Timothy 1:15).

However you may wish to express it, this Communion tells a story that happened *for you*, and in a sense, *to you*. So make this a time of personal fellowship with Jesus Christ. **Call**

Him *your* Savior and *your* Lord, and rejoice in His love for *you*.

Prayer

Our Father, how easy it is for us to let our worship become an impersonal thing! Even so precious an occasion as the Lord's Supper can become an empty, mechanical form. Let this hour of worship become warm and personal and filled with meaning. In Jesus' name, amen.

'Tis Midnight; and on Olive's Brow

(Hymn 321)

Scripture Reading: Luke 22:39-46

Our television sets of some twenty years ago carried an unusual historical series entitled

"You Are There," hosted by the late Edward R. Murrow. The series depicted famous historical events as they might have been presented in television news programs, had television existed in their times. Through "up-to-the-minute reporting" and "on-the-spot interviews" with people involved in those events, the show gave viewers a sense of "being there."

In different fashion, but just as effectively, William B. Tappan takes us to the garden of Gethsemane as our Savior prayerfully readies himself for the ordeal of the cross.

The first stanza of the hymn helps us to feel the solitude and quietness of the place where "the suff'ring Savior prays alone." The apostles are nearby, but loneliness overwhelms Him who must by himself bear man's sins on Calvary.

In stanza two Mr. Tappan enables us to see the Savior as He "wrestles lone with fears." How easily we forget that Jesus the Son of God was also Son of man and that His dread of the agony and humiliation that lay before Him was very human!

When we sing in stanza three, "The Man of Sorrows weeps in blood," we recall Luke's statement that "his sweat was as it were great drops of blood falling down to the ground" (Luke 22:44). The suffering in Gethsemane was not only mental and spiritual, but very much physical as well.

If it were not for the fourth stanza, with its description of the angels' ministry to Jesus as He prayed, this hymn would leave us with a terrible sense of gloom and grief. But that angelic support apparently gave our Savior the extra strength needed to face the approaching mob, to leave the garden a captive, and to tread those final steps that ended at the cross.

Prayer

Our Father, as we partake of these blessed emblems, help us to remember Calvary, and let us also remember the bitter moments in Gethsemane that went before. In Jesus' name, amen.

First and Last

Scripture Reading: Revelation 22:13

Early in the book of Revelation, the Lord God Almighty is quoted by John as saying, "I am the Alpha and the Omega, . . . which is, and which was, and which is to come." In two subsequent verses, the Lord Jesus ascribes these very titles to himself. And in verse 1:17 Jesus calls himself "the First and the Last," a title used in Isaiah to refer to God. Jesus Christ, our host here at the table of remembrance, is not a mere martyr making sure His followers won't forget His name. He is "the image of the invisible God." He is the Lamb of God who takes away the sin of the world. He is the resurrection and the life, the Holy and Righteous One, the power and wisdom of God, the Lord of all, the Word of God. Add to those titles the glorious names of the Old Testament—Wonderful Counsellor, Mighty God, Everlasting Father,

Prince of Peace, and the suffering servant of Isaiah 53.

This powerful Son of God, full of majesty and glory, graciously invites you and me to eat with Him. It would be a singular honor to dine with the President or with the Queen of England, but the ultimate joy is dining with God! When we commune around the Lord's table, the One by whom, through whom, and for whom all things are made lovingly sets a place at His table for every believer!

Now there are two conditions for receiving an invitation to dine with the Divine: faith in Jesus Christ as Lord and Savior, and the humble confession that we are not qualified to be there. We cannot buy a ticket to Communion; we cannot sup with the Lord Jesus because we are rich, or intelligent, or because we have political clout. The One who called himself the First and the Last once said, "the last shall be first, and the first will be last" (Matthew 20:16, *NIV*). The people who get into the kingdom of God are not the high and the mighty, the proudly religious, or the power brokers. Jesus says that the first (by worldly standards) will be last (by the standards of His kingdom). The last (the committed, cross-carrying believers) will be the first (in the rewards of the kingdom).

Prayer

Father, thank You for Christ Jesus and for the invitation to commune here at His table now, and later at the marriage supper of the Lamb. In His precious name, amen.

Giving and Taking

Scripture Reading: John 10:17, 18

Our Lord is a giver because He is a lover. Love is always seeking ways to give itself away for others. Jesus said that nobody really took His life; He gave it willingly for the sins of the world. He laid down His life. He could have escaped under cover of darkness and gone away to the safety of Egypt or Damascus, but

He stayed and, "like a lamb to the slaughter," went to the cross.

The natural man is a taker. He wants what is coming to him, and more. He wants to be served and coddled and satisfied. Even many Christians are professional takers, knowing little about praising God and much about asking Him for wants.

John does not mention the Lord's Supper, but he does say that at the Passover feast Jesus got up from the meal, wrapped a towel around His waist, and began to wash the dusty feet of His disciples. In a sense, the real symbols of the Christian faith are a towel and a basin. Jesus came into the world not to be served but to serve, and He humbled himself to be their servant. He hoped that the example of His giving would become their lifestyle.

Jesus said, "I am the living bread that came down from heaven. If a man eats of this bread, he will live forever. This bread is my flesh, which I will give for the life of the world."

Giving comes from loving. Taking comes from selfishness. The pattern of life for the Christian ought to be (1) taking from God all that He wishes to provide us in our weakness; (2) giving to others our best service in the spirit of love.

Here at the Communion time, we have a supreme opportunity to examine ourselves as to our giving and taking.

Prayer

Father in Heaven, I will serve You because I love You. You have given life to me. Through Christ my Lord, amen.

Backward and Forward

Scripture Reading: 1 Corinthians 11:26

The Communion of the Lord's Supper is a worship opportunity to look back to the cross of Calvary. Our Lord said, "Do this in remembrance of me." Jesus did not ask His disciples to remember only what He said. He wanted them to remember together the central act of love, His death on a Roman cross for our sins.

Memory can be dulled, and it can become easy to forget. That is one reason we observe birthdays and anniversaries, and why we erect monuments and set aside special holidays like the birthdays of famous leaders or the recollection of military victories. As we sit at the Lord's table and hold in our hands the piece of broken bread and the cup of grape juice, we are reminded that we are saved not by silver and gold but by the precious blood of Christ. The Communion of the Lord's Supper anchors us in the essential truth that God loved the world and gave His only begotten Son to die as the perfect sacrifice for sin. At the table of remembrance we look backward to the cross.

But it is a grave error to look at the Lord's Supper as merely a commemoration. It is a table, not a tomb. We are not meeting together just to be reminded of poor Jesus who was betrayed and killed and sealed up in a cemetery, period. The Christ who is our host at the Communion broke loose from the power of death and burst forth in the glory of resurrection!

To the old Hebrews, "to remember" did not mean just to recall an event or fact. It did not mean cold memorializing. It was a celebration of something meaningful, something so real that it was not just a relic of the past but a living fact and truth for the present. From the pristine church, the Lord's Supper has been a time of joyful celebration and thanksgiving (Eucharist), not a sad, sorry commemoration of a dead Savior. The cross is empty. The Lord is risen!

In the Communion we look backward to the cross, but forward to the triumphant moment when the Lord Jesus comes in power and great glory: "You proclaim the Lord's death until He comes." So the Lord's Supper is an experience of remembering and celebrating and anticipating!

Prayer

According to Thy gracious Word,
In meek humility,
This will I do, my dying Lord,
I will remember Thee. Amen.

Friends and Enemies

Scripture Reading: Matthew 26:21

The enemies of Jesus began to close in for the kill. The forces of evil conspired to do away with the man whom they called an impostor.

Judas Iscariot made a deal for thirty silver coins to turn the Lord Jesus over to the authorities. When the going got rough, Peter would vehemently deny he knew Jesus. The other disciples would be holed up somewhere in Jerusalem during the crucifixion of their Lord, leaving only one, John, to be there when Christ needed them. Yet these are the men He invited to eat the Passover meal with Him in the upper room, the night before the cross.

He had said to them earlier, "Greater love has no one than this, that one lay down his life for his friends. . . . You are my friends." (John 15:13, 14, *NIV*). There they were sitting at the table with Him, weak and vacillating, and He called them His friends. But one there would betray Him before the night was over. The one who dipped his hand into the same bowl with Jesus sold him out for a sack of bribe money. He had spent three years listening to Jesus' sermons. He had seen the miracles as an eyewitness. But within a few hours, Judas the friend would become Judas the enemy.

When believers gather to celebrate the Communion of Jesus' body and blood, the friends and enemies are there. There are potential deniers and betrayers. There are those Paul writes about in Philippians: "Many live as enemies of the cross of Christ. Their destiny is destruction, their god is their stomach, and their glory is in their shame. Their mind is on earthly things." When we use our Christian freedom as an excuse for sensuality, we are enemies of the Lord. We are enemies if we piously take the bread and cup on Sunday and eat at the table of the devil on Monday.

The Lord's Supper is a time to examine ourselves before we drink of the cup of the Lord. It is a high moment to confess our sins and acknowledge that apart from Him we can do nothing. If we are not to become His enemies, we must be diligent about keeping our friendship with Him constantly in repair. We are His friends if we do what He commands.

Prayer

Father God, help us to be faithful unto death, never to betray by word or deed the Lord who has called us friends. For His sake, amen.

Broken and Healed

Scripture Reading: Matthew 26:26

Just after the Passover meal had been eaten by the Lord and His disciples, Jesus made use of the two elements of food that best symbolized His life: bread and wine. But Jesus didn't place all the importance on the elements themselves. The vital meaning is not in bread, but *broken* bread; not in wine, but *poured-out* wine.

Two disciples walked on the road to Emmaus. They were joined by a stranger with whom they conversed all the way home. But when He broke bread for them at the evening meal, they recognized Him as the risen Lord.

Alexander Campbell writes in *The Christian System*, "The loaf must be *broken* before the saints partake of it. Jesus took a loaf from the paschal table and *broke* it before He gave it to His disciples. They received a *broken* loaf, emblematic of His body once whole, but by His own consent broken for His disciples. In eating it we then remember that the Lord's body was by His own consent broken or wounded for us." The broken bread illustrates the brokenness of His body on the cross.

In the brokenness of Jesus Christ we are mended, healed, made whole. That clear Messianic prophecy in Isaiah 53 says it best: "He was pierced for our transgressions, he was crushed for our iniquities; the punishment that brought us peace was upon him, and by his wounds we are healed." By the breaking of His body and the loss of His lifeblood, believers are spiritually healed and reconciled to God.

The Communion hour is not a time for general devotional thoughts. It is a time for us to hold in our hands and place in our mouths those poignant symbols of His brokenness: the grain of the field crushed and pulverized into flour for nourishment and life; the grapes trampled and squeezed until the blood-red juice flows. It is a time to concentrate on the Son of God who loved us and gave himself for us.

Prayer
>Thy body, broken for my sake,
>My bread from Heaven shall be;
>Thy testamental cup I take,
>And thus remember Thee. Amen.

One and All

Scripture Reading: 1 Corinthians 11:29

Paul wrote First Corinthians to people who needed some correction. The Corinthian church had problems, and one of them centered around the Communion. The church had a weekly love feast—a type of carry-in dinner, in the framework of which a Communion service was held. But the Corinthian church had turned it into an eating and drinking orgy. The rich would bring more than enough and eat it up while the poorer Christians would stand around hungry.

Paul berated them for their bad Table manners and accused them of despising the church of God. His two main criticisms were that they had divisions at the Lord's table, the very place where their unity should have been clearly demonstrated, and that they went through the motions of outward form but their spirit was wrong. "It is not the Lord's Supper you eat," said Paul. It was not a corporate act of worship in which the total congregation partook; it was a selfish, sinful desecration.

Paul warned them that anybody who partakes of the bread and wine of the Lord's Supper without recognizing or "discerning the body of the Lord" is going to bring judgment on himself. This probably means that such a person does not understand the nature of the church, the body of Christ, in which there is simply no place for selfishness and unconcern for fellow Christians. These people disregarded their oneness in Christ; as a result, gluttony, drunkenness, and snobbery permeated their meetings like the sewage of Corinth.

When we come to Communion with others, our behavior is important to the Lord. We are not merely on a solo rendezvous with Jesus; we are taking part in a family meal for the glory of the Lord. We cannot dare to commune with others with grudges, jealousies, anger, or unforgiveness in our hearts. That is disastrous and brings judgment on us, making us weak and sick. "A man ought to examine himself before he eats of the bread and drinks of the cup."

Prayer

Forgive us, O God, when we come to Communion unprepared. Create a new heart in us, and renew a right spirit within us, for Jesus' sake. Amen.

Victory and Defeat

Scripture Reading: Romans 8:35, 37

When the church assembles for corporate Communion, it ought to be a victory celebration. The paradox of the Christian gospel is that by the time the sun went down on Good Friday, Jesus had won His victory over the forces of evil. The resurrection of the third day was the essential sequel that made the victory total, but He conquered in the cross. Christ has made a symbol of triumph out of an instrument of execution.

In the cross, Jesus Christ has defeated the devil and death. Those who commit themselves to Him by faith share in His finished victory. We Christians are on the winning side, and cannot ever be ultimately defeated.

But not only do we share in His finished victory. We also continue to share the unfinished conflict. The victory is won, but the mopping-up operations will continue until He comes. "In the world you shall have tribulation," He told His disciples. Christians are not immune from the moral and spiritual struggle, for evil still has some life in it, like the swishing tail of a dying dragon. Paul acknowledges that the church faces trouble, hardship, persecution, famine, nakedness, danger, and sword. But he affirmed that faithful believers are "more than conquerors" through Christ. He was convinced that neither death nor life could separate us from the love of God.

Christians suffer, Christians get sick, Christians are bereaved, Christians are imprisoned, Christians get hurt. The world calls that defeat, but we know these are par for the course for this world, in which Satan still is trying to devour and destroy. In spite of the continuing conflict in evangelizing the world, we know that the victory of God is complete and the outcome is sure. We can face tomorrow with hope, for we know the Lord God omnipotent reigns!

Prayer

Father, here at the Communion all of us praise You for the conquering Christ who disarmed the powers and authorities, triumphing over them by the cross. In the Name above every other name, amen.

Life and Death

Scripture Reading: Romans 5:10

Through the death of Jesus Christ on the cross, those who believe and obey are saved, forgiven, and reconciled to God. Man could not become good enough by keeping commandments and trying to be morally and ethically clean. Because of the grace and love of God and the sacrifice of His Son, we come out of darkness into light, out of despair into hope, out of death into life.

The *death* of Christ is central to the gospel, but the *life* of Jesus Christ is also vital to the Christian: "How much more, having been reconciled, shall we be saved through his life!" wrote Paul. When we become Christians we are brought to God through the atoning death of the Son, and we share in His life as He lives in us as Lord.

The Christian is one who shares Christ's resurrected life and spiritual power. Paul wrote, "He who unites himself with the Lord is one with him in spirit." To another church he wrote, "When Christ, who is your life, appears, then you also will appear with him in glory."

Here at the Lord's table, we are not a sorry lot of disciples abandoned by their Master! Christ is in us, the hope of glory. Our bodies are temples of the Holy Spirit. We have died to the old life and have put on the new life in Christ. This is perfectly illustrated in Christian baptism. We are lowered into the water in a pantomime of dying, being buried, and being resurrected to life. "If we died with Christ, we believe that we shall also live with him. . . . Count yourselves dead to sin but alive to God in Christ Jesus."

One time a little girl, about to be baptized with her parents, impatiently asked, "When are we going to be crucified?" She was not using the proper word, but her understanding was on target!

"I have been crucified with Christ and I no longer live, but Christ lives in me" (Galatians 2:20, *NIV*).

Prayer

Father, thank You for the death of Your Son through whom we have life. In His name, amen.

Absence and Presence

Scripture Reading: Matthew 28:20

Jesus took His disciples up to the Mount of Olives just east of Jerusalem, and there the risen Christ ascended into the heavens before their wide-open eyes. He had just spent forty days with them, proving that He was alive and well, and preparing them for His departure. In

Acts 1 Luke tells us that after the ascension, the disciples stood looking intently into the sky and were reassured by two angels that He would be back.

Even though they saw Him leave, the early church never really felt He was far away. They believed He was going to come back again someday, but they also were convinced He was with them always. Especially when they met together to break the bread of Communion, the disciples believed in His presence. They believed He was at the right hand of God making intercession for us, but they also counted on His companionship, as when Paul prayed for the Ephesians, "that Christ may dwell in your hearts through faith."

Through the years, Christians have been convinced that the Lord is with us in the Holy Spirit of God. Just prior to the cross, Jesus said to the disciples, "It is for your good that I am going away. Unless I go away, the Counselor [Holy Spirit] will not come to you; but if I go, I will send him to you" (John 16:7, *NIV*). Christ lives in us through the Spirit who enables and empowers the church. He is the Comforter, the Paraclete (one who stands beside us). He guides and strengthens the body of Christ and sensitizes us to the living presence of the visibly absent Lord.

The Christ is also present when believers gather for prayer and study of the Word. Jesus said, "Where two or three come together in my name, there am I with them" (Matthew 18:20).

But at no time is the Lord Jesus more real and more present than when the church gathers to celebrate the Communion of the Lord's Supper. No priest, pastor, or preacher changes the common bread and wine into the actual body and blood of Christ, but the Son is truly present as the resurrected host, dwelling by faith in the hearts of the faithful.

Prayer

Thank You, Father, that Jesus is with You in the glory of Your throne room and with us in the reality of Communion. Through Him we pray, amen.

Performance and Participation

Scripture Reading: 1 Corinthians 10:16

The Communion of the Lord's Supper is not a performance.

The early Christians did not sit passively and watch one person enact repetitious movements and read a set of prescribed statements. But from the fifth century onward, the simple Communion of the first century became increasingly clericalized. By the middle ages it was something done by the priest with the people having virtually no part. Worship was traditionally something *one* man did *for* the people instead of something the leader and the congregation did together.

The Communion is not a *performance,* but a *participation.* The Lord's Supper is a *sharing* in the body and blood of Jesus Christ, binding many Christians into one. Paul wrote, ''Because there is one loaf, we, who are many, are one body, for we all partake of the one loaf" (1 Corinthians 10:17, *NIV*).

Thus Communion has both a vertical and a horizontal dimension. In the vertical we each commune with the living God, meditating on His love, confessing our sins to a forgiving Father, praising Him in our hearts, and remembering that each of us is one for whom Christ died. In the horizontal dimension we commune together, sharing in the benefits of His broken body and shed blood.

For centuries the great debate of the theologians was about whether or not anything happens to the bread and wine. Paul is more concerned with what happens to the people partaking. There at the Communion table, he says, we Christians are never more completely one people, one body, one family, in the Lord.

The many members of the body of Christ have diverse gifts, different languages, various skin colors, and other marks of distinction. But at the table of remembrance we participate in the body and blood of our one Lord. He becomes the focus of our unity, and we become closer than any natural relatives.

Prayer

O God, here at the Communion table let me rendezvous with my Lord and be gratefully aware of my brothers and sisters nearby, with whom I share in Jesus. In His name, Amen.

Cross and Resurrection

Scripture Reading: Revelation 1:18

Jesus Christ, the Son of God, who was without sin and who went about doing good, was put to death by the Romans, by the Jews, by you and me. The cross was the result of my sin, Judas' betrayal, Caiaphas' and Annas' wheeling and dealing, Pilate's cowardice, and Satan's shenanigans. But let us not fail to realize that it was also the mighty act of God: "He . . . did not spare his own Son, but gave him up for us all" (Romans 8:32, *NIV*).

The episode of the cross is not about a helpless God unable to do anything to save His Son from a shameful death. It is about God giving His only begotten Son because of love for us sinners. Here at the table is no place and time for us to be mournful. It is a time of joy and thanksgiving. We can actually rejoice and give thanks that Jesus died!

The twin truth of the gospel is that Christ was raised from death in the power and glory of the resurrection! There is no gospel without this historic fact. God's Son died, but now lives! And because He lives we will live also!

The resurrection is not merely the escape of Jesus from the sealed tomb, however. It involves more than the stories of His appearance to Mary and Peter, and Thomas, and the two men on the Emmaus road. The resurrection means that you and I are already living in eternal life, that we have within us the same power that God used to raise Jesus from the dead. The resurrection means that we are the community of the living in the midst of a dying world. The resurrection of Jesus Christ means that the grip of death has been broken, and we need have no fear or apprehension. "Death has been swallowed up in victory. Where, O death, is your victory? Where, O death, is your sting?" (1 Corinthians 15:54, 55, *NIV*)

Lord, by the stripes which wounded Thee,
From death's dread sting Thy servants free,
That we may live and sing to Thee!
   Alleluia!

Prayer

Praise Your holy name, O God, for the grace and love that sent Jesus into the world to die for us sinners! Thank You that He lives, and that He is the Resurrection and the Life! Amen!

Law and Grace

Scripture Reading: Romans 6:14

A fifteen-year-old Hasidic Jew was on his first long journey from home. His flight would take him from London to America and a term in Hebrew school. He was polite but aloof, and declined to shake hands with the Gentiles on either side of him. He wore a battered black hat over his short-cropped hair, complemented by a black suit and black tie. When the stewardess served dinner, she brought him a special kosher meal complete with a form letter from the chief rabbi in London certifying that it was indeed kosher. Before he would unwrap the sealed knife, fork, and spoon, he unbuckled his seat belt and went to see the leader of his group to make sure the use of such utensils would not defile him. He had been taught to refuse conversation about Jesus, for his religious prejudices were galvanized.

Our Lord disliked legalism. He got along with tax collectors, prostitutes, and other sinners. But He was always clashing with Pharisees, scribes, and other religious legalists. Mere observance of the law of morals and ethics is not sufficient. Jesus said He came not to destroy the law but to fulfill it—to make obedience to God not a cold, fearful knuckling under but a glad response of a new spiritual heart.

There is no virtue in the ritual of Communion minus wholehearted worship in spirit and in truth. Christianity is not only a religion, but a relationship. It is the dynamic relationship between a gracious God and a person of faith. The Lord's Supper is not a legalistic institution but a personal and corporate meeting between the church and its living Lord. It is not a matter of speaking the proper liturgical words or observing prescribed sittings and standings. It is a loving and intimate act of thanksgiving to and fellowship with the Lord Jesus.

The boy on the plane was locked into legalism. How sad not to know the joy and freedom of Messiah Jesus, who came to save His people from their sins.

"Love is the fulfillment of the law" (Romans 13:10, *NIV*).

Prayer

Thank You and praise You, Father, that we are not bound by law that we cannot keep, but justified by faith in Jesus Christ, the Righteous One. We worship You through His name! Amen.

Meditations for Special Days

The Best Friday
(Good Friday)

Scripture Reading: John 15:12, 13

The Scriptures tell us that when the soldier pierced the side of Jesus on Calvary, blood and water flowed from His body. The German theologian, Dietrich Bonhoeffer, suggests that these elements represent the two great ordinances of the church. The water reminds us of Christian baptism and the blood brings to mind the Lord's Supper.

From the Old Testament we learn that the concepts of life and the forgiveness of sins were closely associated with the idea of blood. The Jews were forbidden by law to drink blood because life was seen to exist in the blood. As a sacrifice for the remission of their sins, an animal had to be slain and bled before the offering was acceptable.

There is no logical reason given us why the

blood of the innocent must be shed for the guilty. The Communion service simply reminds us again of "the Lamb of God, which taketh away the sin of the world."

Prayer

Father, we recognize that if this Friday hadn't been so bad for Your Son, it wouldn't have been so good for us. Thank You for giving us the best of everything. Amen.

Spring—A Time to Come Alive

(Resurrection Day)

Communion

Scripture Reading: Romans 6:1-5

The sun rises in the east and sets in the west. The early Norsemen had the idea that spring arose each year from the East, and so they called their goddess of spring "Easter." What was once a pagan holiday, celebrating the resurrection of spring, was taken over by Christians to celebrate the resurrection of their Savior.

Perhaps it is significant that Christ died and arose in the springtime of the year. It is at this special time of the year that much of God's creation awakens from its winter dormancy and comes alive again. Jesus, too, seems to come alive again for us at this time of year.

While we usually think about *His* resurrection at Easter time, we should also think about our own resurrection. Perhaps our faith, hope, and optimism have been buried for a long time. Perhaps the happy years we knew as children have been covered over by years of hard work, disappointments, worries, and problems.

Our meditation around this table of Easter memories can resurrect a better self for us, a self that can enjoy again the promise of a new birth! Risen hopes! A risen Savior!

Prayer

Father, help us cling to life—Your life. Keep

us from the humdrum satisfaction of day-to-day ordinariness. Wake us up again and give us the feeling of the new birth! In Jesus' name, amen.

Mothers in Communion
(Mother's Day)

Scripture Reading: Ecclesiastes 11:1

The New Testament was not written about a mother, but about a mother's son. This makes the Christmas story both a human and a divine event.

When Simeon prophesied about Jesus, he told Mary, "A sword shall pierce through thy own soul also" because of this boy. Thirty-three years later, when she looked up at her son on the cross, she understood fully what Simeon had meant. But when we last read of Mary in the Bible, it is after Jesus' ascension into Heaven. She is waiting in Jerusalem with the disciples, praying with them in an upper room.

We do not know what our little baby boys and girls will bring us. Some will bring us a resurrection of great joy. Others will bring us a Calvary full of pain and sorrow. But all mothers today find their real strength at the Lord's table. Christ turned His mother's feelings of sorrow to joy—a transformation that can still take place in all of us.

Prayer

Father, most of us have not lost a son as Mary did, but we have all lost some things that have left us grieving as she must have. Above all things we have lost our innocence and our purity. The sadness of our own blemished condition causes us to cry out for a new beginning and a renewed sense of joy. Keep before us the memory of Jesus' mother, who gave up so much and then discovered so much. In Christ's name, amen.

Remembering an Old Birthday

(Pentecost)

Scripture Reading: Acts 2:1-4

Today is the birthday of the church! For almost twenty centuries, Christians have celebrated that special day when the church was established on Pentecost.

With the passing of time things change. We need only look again at our wedding pictures or the old family album to know how true this is. The church, however, is remarkably similar to what it was on its first birthday. It still shares its money with the poor and needy. It still meets on the "eighth day of the week" (as the Lord's day was sometimes referred to then). And it still observes the Lord's Supper as one of the central elements of Christian worship.

Most parents have known the overwhelming feeling of nostalgia when, after many years, they see again their child's favorite toy or blanket. Instantly the past is present and all the old feelings and thoughts are there! The emblems of the loaf and the cup were among the few physical things that meant anything to Jesus. As we handle and partake of them they bring back the old feelings and treasured memories of Him. As we remember Him we forget ourselves. This remembrance is the best gift we can bring Him on this birthday of the church. This is why He said, "Do this in remembrance of me."

Prayer

Father, it is difficult to give something to someone who has everything, but we also know that all You have ever wanted from us is our love and devotion. Help us, then, to give You that which does not make us poorer but makes us rich indeed. Help us to give up our foolish preoccupation with ourselves and give You the best gift we can give—our trust, our obedience, and our gratitude! Amen.

Thanks for the Memories
(Memorial Day)

Scripture Reading: Hebrews 12:1, 2

We tend to remember our good experiences more clearly than we do our bad ones. It is perhaps fortunate that God made us this way.

Some have wondered why we bring to mind in the Communion service the ugly and painful memory of Jesus' crucifixion. "Why don't we select some happier moment in His life to remember at the Lord's table?" some ask.

At the Lord's table we remember the one thing most worth remembering in Jesus' life. We do not remember Him as a miracle worker or even as a great teacher. We do not remember Him for His wisdom or even for His religion. We remember Him as one who had compassion for a sinful and selfish world. We remember that He gave up His own life so that we might inherit a better one for ourselves.

This is worth remembering more often than just on Sundays! We start with Sunday and hope that by the end of the week we will still be giving thanks for the wonderful memories.

Prayer
Our Father in Heaven, give us good memories for the things that count. Keep us from nursing old wounds and bad memories of ourselves and others. Keep before our minds the sweet thought of Your marvelous grace. In Jesus' name, amen.

Coming Home
(Homecoming Day)

Scripture Reading: Matthew 18:12-14

We have all heard or read the story in the Bible about the prodigal son. It is a story about a boy who left his home for pleasures elsewhere. Most people think that the main lesson in the story is the boy's behavior; a young man enters into sin, finally comes to his senses, and then, at last, returns to his father.

The main focus of the story, however, is not the son—it is the father! He is standing at the door waiting for his son's return. He had given instructions to the servants that should his son return, they should welcome him with open arms.

There is nothing so terrible that we could ever do, nor is there any depth to which we could ever sink, that would cause our heavenly Father's concern and love for us to wear thin or disappear. This homecoming day should be a day in which all Christians seriously evaluate what journeys they might have taken away from God this year and whether or not they have fully returned and recovered from them.

The Communion service can be a helpful signpost pointing the way to God. It can give us an idea of just how far we have strayed from God's road, and of how far we have yet to travel in our pilgrimage back to God.

Prayer

Sometimes we wonder, Lord, whether we have wandered too far away from You to return. Some of us have felt homesick at times for the wonderful experiences we used to have when we were more faithful in our Christian lives. What a wonderful feeling it is to be with the family of God. Help us to know again that there's no place like home. In Christ we pray. Amen.

Leaving the Table Empty
(Thanksgiving)

Scripture Reading: Psalm 95:1, 2

"And he took the cup, and gave thanks, and gave it to them, saying, Drink ye all of it."

While Jesus was giving thanks, Judas was betraying Him, Peter was soon to deny Him, James and John were about to fall asleep on Him, and the Romans and Jews were searching the city so they could rid society of Him. It takes a great man to be thankful in the face of much good, but it takes God to be thankful in the face of so much bad.

Jesus was not as thankful for His extremities as He was for His opportunities. We sometimes have the idea that when we are reduced to nothing, we have nothing and are nothing. Jesus suggested that when we are reduced to nothing we have everything, because it is then that we recognize more fully that we have God. His encouragement to us is that we should empty ourselves so we can be full of God and full of good.

The Lord's table is not designed to fill us up, but to empty us. Most of us bring ourselves to the table full of pride and self-conceit. When we partake of these emblems, we seek to empty ourselves of these harmful qualities. This is truly a Thanksgiving meal! It can humble us and make us empty. It is the only way for us to become completely full-filled.

Prayer
Father, fill us with a great urge to be empty! Take away the qualities that deplete us. Give us a daily readiness to start all over again with a simple trust in You. Thank You for second and third helpings of Your grace. Amen.

Bringing Christmas and Easter Together
(Christmas)

Scripture Reading: Luke 2:34, 35

At this point in our worship service we are faced with what might appear to be a contradiction in purpose and meaning. This is Christmas Sunday; our thoughts are centered around Christ's birth. The Lord's Supper or Communion service, on the other hand, reminds us of Christ's death. But Christ's death is more of an

Easter event than a Christmas one!

Still, the contradiction is not a real one. There was no room for Him at the inn, but there was plenty of room for Him on the cross. His birth was in an ugly place, and so was His death. A star came to brighten His birth, but the lights went out completely at his death. He was born in a borrowed manger, and He was buried in a borrowed tomb.

There is a great correspondence between these two events in Jesus' life. We cannot understand one without understanding the other. Through the emblems of the loaf and the cup, we emphasize the end of His life in order to gain a better perspective as we view the beginning of it on Christmas Sunday.

Prayer

Father, it is the child in each of us that thanks You for Christmas and all its joy and magic. But it is the adult in each of us, Father, that thanks You for Easter. What peace and contentment there is to know we are forgiven for the hurt we too often bring You! Joyously and gratefully we thank You for Christmas and Easter. Amen.